Donut Destiny

Nicole Walton

Made with ❤ on the BookLeaf Publishing Platform
www.bookleafpub.in
www.bookleafpub.com

Dedication

To myself, for finding the strength to pick up the pieces.
And to him, for being both my muse and my lesson.

Preface

I wasn't a poet before this.
When pain hits, you find ways to expel it.
For me, that meant turning old memories
into new pieces of art—
each one an exit for the heaviness
that had nowhere else to go.

These pieces reveal a part of my side.
Imposter syndrome left behind,
masterpiece be damned.
This was about survival,
about making sense of what felt like senseless loss.

By the end,
I was sick of him living in my head,
of the weight I gave to someone
who had already walked away.

This is how I set him down—
line by line, word by word,
until the only thing left
was my own reflection.

Keep in mind, there are two sides to every story.

Realities seldom align perfectly.
But this is my truth:
my love, my failure, my rebuild.

Acknowledgements

To the friends who listened without judgment,
and the family who stood beside me even when I felt lost
—

thank you for your patience and love.
And to this process—thank you for giving me a place to
put it all.

As Old As Time

When they first met,
he thought she was funny—
in a way he couldn't quite define.
She thought he was charming,
but couldn't fathom why her rambling stories
held his attention.

They hadn't met in person yet.
Business calls stretched deep into the night,
their voices tangling through hours of hesitation and
connection.

He admired her honesty,
her unpolished openness,
the way she let him into her world
as if she had never been hurt.
She admired his restraint,
how his quiet facade
masked a tenderness he revealed sparingly—
each disclosure deliberate,
each moment a gift.

Together, they began to see each other
in ways neither had been seen before.

He hated her clashing colors,
her mismatched boldness daring the world to notice her.
She resented his manicured hair,
his polished car—
a pristine illusion that felt distant, unreachable.
Time softened their edges—
her chaos became charm;
his precision became poetry.

He feared loving her,
afraid that her disorder
would unravel the meticulous world he had built.
But she taught him that beauty lives
not in perfection,
but in its absence.

She didn't know how to fall gently,
but with him,
the hollow spaces she thought unfillable
began to heal.

Love was magnetic,
inevitable.
Not a choice—
but a force, unstoppable.

When they kissed,

it wasn't just an introduction.

It was a collision—

their walls crumbling as they unwound one another,

like a clockwork spell

set into motion

by the rhythm of their connection.

Rain Monopoly

The rain traces the window, slow, deliberate—
Muffled sounds of the register and a polite "thank you"
pull me back to you.
Your hand rests on my waist, guiding me gently toward
the door,
a softness between us,

But then you walk, slow, measured,
through the rain, guarding the pies like they're the only
thing you own.
Everyone else runs, hurrying to shield themselves from
the storm—
but you just walk, unhurried, unbothered.
Letting your guard down, allowing the world to see you,
but everyone was too preoccupied to notice.
The rain, your shield into being seen.

We're miles away from anywhere,
in the mountains, where the world feels distant, as if we
are the only two people here,
and for a moment, the rush of everything stops.

When you turn, surprised, I am still here, outside the
little shop,

the world washed out by rain.
Your smile tilts, playful,
and I wonder—
Could we dance here?
In the rain, with no music playing,
lost in the kind of fiction we were—
but the quiet between us made it feel real.

First Kiss

A misunderstanding,
not the first, not the last.
Under the table,
I find your feet,
massaging them—a quiet apology.

We aren't angry at each other,
but at ourselves—
letting fantasy cloud the truth
of what we are.
Trying to contain something
that refuses to be defined.

Your hair untamed,
you crawl across the floor,
playful, silly,
closing the gap between us
in your own way.

On opposite sides of the table,
we meet in the middle.
Close now—so close.
Faces inches apart,
the air holding its breath.

This kiss will seal our fate.

Taunting each other with the pull,
the push,
a sparring match stretched into eternity.
The decision hangs between us,
too heavy to name,
too light to resist.

And then—
touching lips.
Warmth floods through my hands,
your neck fevered beneath my touch,
your breath mixing with mine,
the faint salt of anticipation shifting,
unfolding into fire,
pulling us into a rhythm
we could never escape.

Your hands find my waist,
pulling me closer.
My legs wrap gently around yours,
the air between us surges—
both scared,
both surrendering.

And so it began,

the weight of us colliding,
unstoppable, undeniable.

Wild by Nature

You made the world feel endless,
like the horizon wasn't an edge,
but a curve daring me to follow.

I watched how you moved—
mocking rules,
rewriting them with ease,
as if you'd been handed the cheat codes to life.
It wasn't arrogance;
it was mastery.
You bent the world to your will,
and I wanted to learn how.

I mirrored your confidence,
trying to match the rhythm of your stride.
But no matter how closely I followed,
my steps always felt borrowed.
You painted visions of a future,
fearless in erasing the past.

In those moments,
you'd pull me into your orbit—
your power not in dominance,
but in the way you held the universe so gently,

inviting me to see it too.

You made me believe I could do anything.
But in the quiet,
I wondered—
was it me you believed in,
or the reflection of yourself in my eyes?

Emotional Intelligence

Emotional intelligence—
a muscle built in dim-lit rooms,
between whispered prayers and unspeakable truths.

Sitting in circles, sharing realities no one dares say aloud.
Each story, a repetition.
Each hour, a thread weaving strength into the fragile.

Therapy sessions, gratitude journals, prayer.
Movements I returned to, again and again,
carving out a space to share what I'd learned.
Lessons rooted in past lives I no longer live.
I think you admired these insights,
how they shed light on things you never saw about
yourself.

Pride, double-sided.
Yours softening, your defenses falling away.
Mine, growing at the chance to bring merit to us—
a balance we didn't know we were building.
Logic, your strong suit;
mine still learning its place.

Yin and yang, flowing through this chapter of life.

Learning, growing.

Doubt hums quietly, like a faint vibration.
This muscle—delicate yet strong—
demands care, demands work.
Neglect makes it stiff, unfamiliar.
The insights I gave—once a gift—
became sharp, cutting where they once healed.
I didn't see it happening.
Maybe neither of us did.

I sit now with what I've learned.
The strength I earned,
the strength I let falter.
It wasn't lost, only dormant—
waiting for hands willing to shape it,
to stretch and tend again.

And this time, I will.

Orange Corduroy

I couldn't make it to bed last night—
the stairs seemed too daunting.
Energy spent on sobs, my spoons depleted.

Limp on the sectional,
I slowly run my fingers over the corduroy.
The fabric's grooves, warmth buried within them,
pull me back to your hands on mine.

Your heat lingers in the folds of the fabric,
like a phantom pressing my fingers deeper still.
Memory strikes of your hands on top of mine,
pushing them into the upholstery—
passionate, primal.

Eyes locked—wordless conversations exchanged
in a language only we could speak,
each glance unveiling something hidden.
Separate identities molding themselves, merging.

You said it was too much.
Too intense.
You had never experienced it that way before.
I didn't know any other way.

What began as a comforting quilt of shared moments
became something frayed,
its edges unraveling under the weight
of what we couldn't say.

You needed air,
and all I could do was drown
in the warmth of us, pressing too close.

The Dance

The bull, once wild, tamed by time and trials,
grazing in green pasture.
Reformed, stronger—
invited to the dance again.

As it enters, shadows of memory stir—
subtle reminders of destruction's path,
of what it is capable.
This time is different. No audience,
no crowd to bear witness.

The matador nods,
a single strand falling perfectly—
deliberate, almost mocking,
an illusion of effortless control.

The flag flutters, red and alive,
adrenaline floods the bull.
Instinct takes over as it barrels forward—
a miss,
its body slamming into the barricade.
Just a scratch, it thinks.
A flesh wound.

The dance continues, fluid and rehearsed—
a song of tragic melody,
each note sharper than the last.
The bull begins to fray,
its shape dissolving into blood and motion.

The bull glances at the empty stands—
now full of calculating eyes,
faces cloaked in navy shadows,
waiting for the finale,
eager for the next victim.

The spear strikes deep, a sharp betrayal,
terms it never knew tearing it apart.
The matador—green eyes flat, hands steady,
untouched by remorse—
pulls the blade free.

The bull collapses.
The flag falls.
The dance is over.

Not Without a Fight

The door slams, reverberating in my chest—
finality I refuse to accept.
In a world of color, you paint only in stark lines—
black against white.
The shadows, the highlights—
I beg you to see them before it's too late,
plead with you to bend,
to shape like clay.

This is big—important,
like the first time our arms brushed,
a jolt of something electric,
the kind of spark you don't forget.
We were magic then,
a force of nature untamed,
and I know we can be that again.

Even you admitted it once—
what we had was more than this ending.
But now your silence frays
the edges of what we built,
unraveling us thread by thread.

You see problems, and they suffocate you.

These are opportunities.
We are better together,
not out of complacency—
but because there's more to learn,
more to build,
if we'd just stand side by side.

We argue, yes,
but this friction sharpens us.
Windows cracked open
so we can peer in,
become something truly great.

Your silence sits in the room, arms crossed,
like peace is found in distance.
I fight against it,
my voice filling the space you've abandoned.

I won't let fear dismantle this.
Not yours, not mine.
We can still rebuild—
if you let me stand beside you.

Crossfire

Dismissal meets petulance,
eye rolls slicing through the stale air.
I can't sit across this desk from you for one more second.
This is a war I never wanted to fight—
disdain crawling up my throat like bile.
No bare flags waving between us,
just silence stretched too thin to hold.

Your manufactured smiles,
brittle as glass,
shattering under my gaze.
My sly remarks,
petty wounds disguised as jokes,
spill into ears eager for division.
A shadow coiled between us,
feeding on our failures,
waiting for its moment to strike.
An enemy to us both.

We've destroyed all paths forward.
No high roads—
just this, the lowest valley,
carved by our silence and blame,
gazing up at the peaks where we once stood,

each accusing the other of the fall.

Fingers pointed like pistols,
each ego pulling the trigger.
Blood stains the desk,
yours and mine.
Defenses raised like iron walls,
impenetrable yet isolating.

Your silence is suffocating,
a wall I can't break.
So I lash out,
cutting through the tension with words that wound—
aggression thinly veiled as truth.
Each jab, each attack,
another scar on something we once cherished.

We could stop this—
call a truce.
But instead, we stand in the rubble—
weapons drawn, flags tattered,
the echoes of what we were
drowned by what we've become.

Last Day

I was frozen at my desk,
tears falling before I could stop them.
I cried at him—
I didn't mean to.
I tried to stop myself, but I couldn't.

He didn't feel the same.
His stare, cold and distant,
carved deeper than words ever could.
I think he pitied me—
but his pity only made it worse.

He was relieved I was leaving—
a guilt he carried lightly,
too shallow to spark a single word of comfort.
And I, broken in front of him,
offered nothing back.

That was it—
the last moment,
the air between us heavy with humiliation,
the weight of goodbye sinking into my chest like stone.

Sunsets on 78

The scenery is breathtaking—
sun rays casting long shadows over the mountains,
their peaks heavy, preparing to rest for the night.

This same commute, once a daily gift, now feels empty—
just a drive, coming from nothing, headed nowhere.
The mountains feel stolen from me,
their beauty obscured by new realities,
clouds groaning like a storm,
pushing shadows over the peak.

I weave through the canyon, hyper-focused—
not because the road is unfamiliar, but because I know it
too well.
The guardrails stand like sentinels—
cold steel against the yawning abyss.
I know their beginning, their end.
I know the gaps where they fail.

My hands grip the wheel tighter
as thoughts creep in, unbidden.
Fast enough, I think.
Accidents happen all the time.
Who would even know?

The weight of these thoughts pulls me under,
and when I finally surface, I'm crying.
Again.
I can't remember the last time I didn't cry on this drive
home.

Tears carve their paths,
soft as water etching stone—
the canyon and I, reshaped by time,
weathered but still standing.

My body floats, weightless,
breath dragging behind.
I don't want to die... do I?
Or am I just waiting to live again?

Soft Anger

Rage rises, heavy as lead,
crawling up through my feet.
I hate him for moving on so fast—
for walking so easily into her arms.

This wasn't a game.
The stakes were high:
my career, my future, my body.
Puppeteered by him,
strings pulled taut,
then snapped in the static of a phone call.

Anger simmers, swelling,
until it meets my heart—
where it stops, collides, softens.
Love, insistent, seeps back in,
its warmth unwelcome.

How could I blame him?
When you meet your person,
you run with them,
unapologetically into the unknown.

It wasn't me.

A bitter pill I try to swallow,
sharp and unyielding.

We all have battles to wade,
burdens to carry.
He sacrificed me to save himself—
a choice I can't call kind,
but maybe necessary.

The brokenness I carry
is no longer his burden.
He is free of me.
And I, of him.
For better or worse.

Illuminated Shame

This iPhone—the instrument I use to flog myself.
Keys worn smooth by the rhythm of obsession,
memorized paths to the life of a stranger.
Each scroll amplifies insecurities,
the room dissolves into static
as a wave of cortisol bursts over me,
like a dam collapsing without warning.

Images bend sound and time,
undulating, rhythmic pulses—
stretching, collapsing,
the world itself buckling under unseen heat.

Each swipe tightens the noose,
until shadows replace the walls.
Darkness presses in,
while the blue light carves hollow shadows across my
face.
Reduced to the silhouette of someone I used to love,
I cling to the suffocating weight of control.

The past overtakes the present,
stripping away dignity and pride.
The reflection I pretend is her—

is really me, whispering truths I don't want to hear:
Her cashmere sweater drapes over a life
I was never meant to wear.

And as the glass reflects my shame,
I wonder—
who will teach me to be whole,
if not her,
if not him,
if not me?

The screen dims,
but I remain illuminated—
not by light,
but by the weight of my shame.

The Hoarder

I've never moved on from anything in my life.
Memories don't fade;
they settle like dust in forgotten corners,
gathering weight until they crumble.
I tell myself I'll sort through them one day—
but the truth is, I can't.

I keep you on a high shelf.
Your laugh, a jar of preserved air.
Your hand in mine,
a rusted key without a lock.
Every room holds pieces of us—
a museum for a story that no longer exists.

This hoard is a burden,
but I don't know how to live without it.
I should clear the shelves,
donate your smile to oblivion,
but my grip tightens every time I try.

I tell myself a new room will replace the old,
that one day you'll be just a relic,
something I can lock away.
But I can still hear you in the walls,

your presence in the cracks,
and I'm afraid to step into the quiet,
where your echoes don't follow.

Donut Destiny

A theory strung together by ordinary people.
Not scientists—
but philosophers in the rain,
exploring the whimsical nuances of life
when it felt safe to wonder out loud.

Everyone is a donut, they decided.
You don't choose the donut you are;
it's handed to you by the divine,
written in the stars we gaze at
while making sense of life with loved ones.

She willed herself to be a bear claw,
but she was a glazed twist—
funky by design,
pulled apart to reveal
the softness of two sides.

He was her beloved maple bar.
Traditional and smooth,
overlooked by those
with unworthy palates,
rich for anyone who took the time
to savor the box.

Together, they were the perfect combo,
casting long shadows over the rest—
two large donuts, bold and unyielding,
nestled on top of every box.

But fate isn't something you choose.
It's designed with purpose.
They thought they'd share a box forever,
but found themselves matched with others—
new fillings,
new lives,
none quite the same.

Now she sits with the memory,
of pulling him apart,
savoring the sweetness inside,
and wonders:
Can you ever truly accept your donut?

They were two donuts,
shared briefly in a box of time.
You don't choose your donut—
only savor what you're given,
then let go when it's gone.

Helium

There are moments when grief hums softly,
when the world doesn't demand answers,
and the moon, full and bountiful,
presses its light gently against the dark.

Tonight, I step barefoot into the grass,
leaving the fire's warmth behind,
its flicker a sacrifice I no longer need.
The night breathes around me—soft, warm,
as though it has been waiting for my return.

My dog watches from the doorway,
his gaze steady and familiar.
Even in his silence, he reminds me:
I have been here before,
and I will be here again.

The wind finds me,
familiar as an old friend,
brushing my cheek,
lifting strands of my hair,
as if to say, look up.
And I do.

The moon hangs above me,
a quiet witness,
its fullness matching the gratitude
that rises in my chest.

I have carried sorrow long enough
to know its weight.
Tonight, it drifts away,
weightless as helium,
leaving me lighter, freer,
tethered only to this moment,
and no longer to my pain.

The tears come—
gentle, cleansing,
not the sobs of despair
but a prayer,
a gift of thanks to the stillness,
to the god of quiet nights,
to the heart that still beats.

I am okay.
In this moment,
that is enough.

Maternal Instinct

I see my mother in him—
in the way he draped confidence over insecurity,
a facade so seamless
you'd miss the cracks
unless you'd lived with them.

Her silence was a distance
I never learned how to cross.
He carried that same quiet pull—
close, then gone,
leaving me to wonder
if the gap was ever mine to bridge.

Her voice taught me to see:
art in the overlooked,
beauty in the broken.
She shaped the world into something extraordinary,
even as she unraveled it.

When he disappeared,
it felt familiar—
the same hollow absence,
the same ache of wanting
to be enough.

Her roots twist deep in me,
guiding my choices
in ways I don't always understand.
She lingers in the shadows I avoid,
in the light I chase,
in the love I give
and the wounds I strive to heal.

Aftermath

The storm came like a thief in the night—
tearing through with reckless hands,
stealing more than it left behind.

I quit the life I'd built,
left the walls I called mine.
Returned to a house I no longer fit,
its walls heavy with the ghosts of who I was,
mocking me from the shadows.

These hands, once carriers of hope,
now hang limp, heavy with dismay.
The same body I offered to you,
lingering, open—
a fragile gift.
The next morning,
I felt the hollow ache
of something taken but left unfinished.

You left me with this:
mud-slick ground,
scattered pieces.
My confidence—
a thing I gave you freely,

now shattered,
its sharp edges cutting into my palms
as I try to hold it.

I am angry.
At you, for the storm.
At myself, for standing still
while you dismantled me.

This rebuilding isn't elegant—
no golden seams mend these cracks.
Just crude repairs,
rough as my resolve.
Brick stacked on brick,
tears and dirt mixing into mortar.

But it's mine.
The first light breaks,
gray and clean,
a quiet possibility
I don't yet believe in.
Yet I remain,
sifting through the wreckage,
shaping what's left
into something wholly mine.

Deep Waters

I'm ready to love again,
to know someone in subtle ways—
nuances that only surface in requited love.

I want to taste my lover,
to dive deep into their waters,
to feel the salt sting my eyes
and the weight of trust pressing against my chest.
No fear, no reservation—
focus dissolving into devotion.

But love is no calm sea.
It demands we navigate the storms,
waves that rise uncalled,
threatening to pull us under.
How many more lives do I have?
How many more wrecks can I survive?

Some things are hard to reconcile—
the cruel joke of love,
the prophecy fulfilled by fear.
But the horizon beckons,
its light stretching over the tide.

There is no knowing,
only the leap.
Trusting myself, my partner,
to guide me to the surface
when the waters rage.

Death by Pearls

I will never wear pearls unironically.
There's grit in my bones—
you can hear it when I dance.

These hands,
formed from the dirt of my upbringing,
carry truth sharpened at the edge of my voice.

My shadow doesn't follow;
it waits,
holding the pieces I've lost,
daring me to look back.

For a moment,
I thought happiness might glow beneath the Eiffel
Tower,
but shadows stretch farther than I imagined,
reaching places I swore they'd never touch.

Keep your white roses.
I thrive where wildflowers split forgotten stone,
where beauty grows untamed,
where edges remain sharp.

I run into the hillsides,
fireflies lighting paths from the dark.

I am not a prize
rooted in sophistication.
I will never wear pearls unironically.

The Last Word

I've carried him long enough.
His memory, once a comfort,
is now a weight I can't afford.

Pain is strange like that—
familiar enough to cling to,
even when you know it's killing you.

I wrote this for me,
but maybe also for the woman
who needs permission
to stop dragging ghosts into the future.

Magic has always been mine to wield.
This body, this voice,
these hands—
they have built and broken
a hundred worlds before this one.
Why not make the next
my masterpiece?

I am tired, but I am ready.
I miss him, and I always will—
but I won't live my life

with his dead body trailing behind me.

This is the first step.
Not clean, not perfect,
but mine.

9 789367 399224